Freelance Writing Entrepreneur: Write and Grow Rich

KEESHA METCALFE

ISBN: 1523711213
ISBN-13: 978-1523711215

DEDICATION

This book is dedicated to my sons Raheem, David-Alexander and Joel

CONTENTS

KEESHA METCALFE

ACKNOWLEDGMENTS

I'd like to thank God for planting this book in my spirit and for giving me the grace to complete it. Thanks also to my husband and sons for their unwavering support while I worked relentlessly to make this book a reality.

INTRODUCTION

Whenever people ask me what I do for a living and I tell them that I'm an online Freelance Writer, many furrow their brows in wonder. Can someone really make a living as an online Freelance Writer? Whenever I get this type of reaction, I smile because just a few years ago I would have had the same reaction if I was the one posing the question. Coming from being a manager within a financial institution to a full time Freelance Writer who has created 4 solid streams of income from my writing, I have come full circle and have done what many said was impossible.

The demand for freelance writers is high. Today I earn a full time income as an online Freelance Writer working from home. They say that the average millionaire has 7 streams of income. I have created 4 from my writing talent and I have written this book to demonstrate how very possible it is for writers to earn a lucrative online income from freelance writing.

In this book, I detail exactly what it takes to make a full time income from writing online and how anyone with a talent for writing can cash in on their talent and the abundant opportunities available online for earning as a writer. You will learn everything that you need to succeed as a freelance writer including:

BONUS: List of 100 Websites that Pay Handsomely for Freelance Writing!

Where to Find Clients

How to Pitch Effectively

Making Passive Income

How to Launch Your Freelance Writing Career

How to Stand Out on Online Platforms

How to Grow Your Freelance Writing Business
Why You Need to Have Your Own Blog
How to Become a Wealthier Freelance Writer
Social Media Marketing for Freelance Writers and much more!

While the information contained in this book will be useful to any Freelance Writer, it is especially targeted to the person who wants to know how to use the internet to make a living as a writer. By investing in this valuable resource, you will be armed with all the information you need to get started with your online writing career. The timing is right. Let's write and grow rich!

SO YOU WANT TO BECOME A FREELANCE WRITER?

Freelance writing has gone the full gamut from simply being something that folks did to supplement their incomes to being a very noble and potentially very lucrative profession. This noble profession has enabled ambitious writers to carve out enviable lifestyles for themselves and for the families that love them and depend on them for daily sustenance.

Would you ever have imagined that a freelance writer could make a full-time income from simply writing? And not just any full-time income either. There are freelance writers out there who are making as much as 6 figures per year and they are doing it from the comfort of their homes. They are doing it while touring the world with their families. They are doing it from anywhere and everywhere that internet services are available. There is a new generation of writers out there who have defied the odds and who have proved the sceptics totally wrong. You CAN make a lucrative income from freelance writing. You can WRITE AND GROW RICH!

I have written this book for those ambitious writers out there who are willing to push the limits to realize their full earning potential doing what they do best – writing! This book is for writers who want to write and grow rich.

If you think about it for a while, you will realize that the idea is not as far-fetched and outlandish as it initially appears. Given the tremendous opportunities that the internet has opened up to the world, it takes only a slight stretch of the imagination to see exactly how possible this is. Gone are the days when writers were at the mercies of publishers to get their work out into the world. Gone are the days of starving writers who could forget about becoming rich from their talents. Long gone and good riddance to them too. This is a new day! Thanks to Amazon and other online book retailers, self-publishing is now a very viable alternative that allows would be best-selling authors to get their work published at a fraction of the time, a fraction of the costs and a fraction of headache associated with traditional publishing. Not only that, but with the growing number of websites going live, the demand for web content is growing exponentially. If you are a freelance writer, your services are definitely in demand. People need well-written content for their websites and many of them are willing to pay top dollars to have talented writers produce that content for them. It's a great time to be a freelance writer!

PASSIVE SOURCES OF INCOME FROM WRITING

Now, more than ever, it is possible to earn multiple streams of passive income from your writing. Personally, I believe that creating passive income streams is the best way to get wealthy as a writer. Not only that, but it is also the type of income that will allow you the greatest level of financial freedom possible – the kind of financial freedom that allows you to sit back, kick up your feet and relax as you listen to the 'kaching' of your money rolling in long after the hard work has ended. We all dream of being able to earn without slaving at some task day in and day out. The beauty about passive income is that you do the hard work up front and then reap the rewards over and over and over again! As a freelance writer, there are several ways to earn passive income. I am about to tell you about 4 different streams of income that you can create online from freelance writing. Namely, by writing and self-publishing print and e-books, blogging, selling online courses, and revenue sharing.

Writing and Self-Publishing Print Books and E-books

Thanks to internet technology, now almost anyone can write and self-publish their own print and e-books and earn royalties. With online marketplaces such as Amazon and Barnes & Noble with their Kindle and Nook publishing options, talented freelance writers can create and earn very lucrative streams of income. At the click of a button, freelance writers can become published authors who can make their work quickly accessible to millions of readers all over the world. All at very, very affordable prices that the average reader is easily able to afford. With e-books being sold for as little as $0.99, writers have a huge database of customers who they can market their e-books to. And people are always looking for great books to read that provide entertainment or information. Amazon alone has a whopping 244 million customers as at December 2015 and there are several other smaller online retailers through which freelance writers can market their books. Published authors can earn very attractive royalties of up to 90% of the list price depending on the platform that their books are sold on. The more books you have self-published as an author, the more royalties you will be able to earn.

Some self-published authors earn very lucrative incomes from their work. Author Mark Dawson has sold 300,00 copies of his fiction book and earns approximately $450,000 per annum from his writing. Other notable authors who have self-published bestsellers include David Chilton, author of the financial planning book, *The Wealthy Barber,* James Redfield, author of *The Celestine Prophecy,* Lisa Genova, author of *Still Alice* and several others. There is absolutely no reason why you shouldn't be able to become a bestselling author yourself. But it doesn't take a best seller to earn a lucrative income from writing. All it takes is the drive to write a good book, and self-publish it. Who knows, you could very well hit the jackpot!!

Many freelance writers are of the mistaken belief that self-publishing requires a lot of technical skills. That is far from the truth. The fact is that self-publishing is one of the easiest aspects of earning income as an author. All you need to do is to write the book using simple word processing software such as Word. There are several other freelancers out there who can format your work in e-book format for as little as $5 on your behalf. Once your book is formatted, all you need to do is to set your price and to upload it to the platforms of choice.

The hardest and most important part of earning royalties from self-publishing a book is marketing it. Unlike traditional publishers who will market your book for you, with self-publishing, all the marketing is on your shoulders. The truth is that it isn't necessarily the best writers who become best sellers. It is those who market their books the best. If marketing doesn't come naturally to you as a freelance writer, understand that it is an essential skill that you have to learn in order to maximize your earnings. Otherwise, you are likely to get lost among the crowd of freelance writers out there. If you are serious about earning passive income from your writing, you should definitely write and self-publish your own books. But make sure that you invest in learning how to market those books once you have written them.

How to actually write your book is beyond the scope of this book. But there are numerous resources out there that will teach you exactly how to go about writing and self-publishing your own books. I highly recommend:

- Chandler Bolt's Self-Publishing School. You will learn everything that you need to know about writing, self-publishing and marketing your very own books. Chandler is a 5-time bestselling author and entrepreneur who was struggling doing odd jobs before he decided to write and publish his own books.

Passive Income from Blogging

Blogging is a special type of content marketing in which subtle, less direct ways are used to offer solutions to readers' problems or to provide information that readers are looking for. A blog allows you to market and advertise several different types of products (related to the blog's niche) while supplying readers with valuable content. The great thing about blogging is that it is very possible that your blog posts will end up in the search engine result pages (SERPs) when people conduct keyword searches online. If they click through to your blog article, if you have provided links to related products in your blog post or have advertised those products using banner ads etc, readers should be able to purchase those products directly from your blog. When they do, you earn passive income. Whether you choose to market affiliate products or to market your own products through blogging, it is a good way to earn passive income from your writing.

Here is an example of how blogging works. Let's say you operate a food blog that focuses on the gluten-free lifestyle. You would write and publish several different articles related to the gluten-free lifestyle. Let's say that you write and publish a review of a great cook-book with easy and delicious gluten-free recipes as a blog post. Within the post, you provide several links that readers can click on to actually purchase the cook book for themselves.

And suppose that someone goes to Google searching for 'gluten-free recipes'. If your blog post comes up in the search results and the reader clicks on it, they will be able to read your review of the cook book and to actually purchase the book straight from your blog if you stimulate their interest enough with your review. If they do so, you would earn revenues, either affiliate income or direct income if you were the writer of the cook book.

Another way that you could earn as a freelance writer from blogging is through Google Adsense. Google Adsense is an advertising program that Google owns that allows advertisers to advertise on approved blogs. These ads would appear at strategic places within the content of your blog. Usually Google only shows ads that are related to the content that you would have produced on your blog. Advertisers pay Google to show their ads on different blogs. Whenever the readers of your blog click on any of these ads, Google would pay you a specific amount. The more your readers click on these ads, the more Adsense revenue you would earn. This is a great source of passive income but you shouldn't expect to get rich from Google Adsense income unless you have several thousands of visitors to your blog on a monthly basis. Nevertheless, it is a good way to earn additional passive income from your writing efforts.

As a blogger, you can also earn income from sponsored posts. A sponsored post is a blog post that a company pays a blogger to write and publish on their blog. The post may take the form of a review of the sponsor's product or it may be a regular blog post with links to the sponsor's products from which readers can purchase products. The sponsoring company usually supplies the blogger with free products for them to use for themselves, after which they would write up a review. This is generally a more lucrative form of earning than Google Adsense and affiliate marketing since a single sponsored blog post can earn a blogger hundreds or even thousands of dollars. The amount that companies are willing to pay is usually dependent on the number of visitors or views that the blog receives monthly as well as the blog's authority and page rank.

If you have not yet started your own blog, I highly recommend my book *"WordPress for Beginners: Simple Guide to Blogging for Profit"* which will show you how to start your very own WordPress blog and how to make income from it.

Selling Online Courses

Nowadays, it is not necessary for students to actually be physically present in a classroom in order to take courses. Thanks to the internet, courses can be taken from wherever there is an internet connection. This is great news for freelance writers who have a love and a knack for writing course material. It means that as a freelance writer, you are able to write your own courses and to sell them online to students all across the world. No longer is the classroom limited by geographical boundaries. Instead, courses may be taken virtually at any time all at the student's convenience. You, as the teacher, also don't have to be physical present to teach a class. In fact, while you are sleeping, students will be able to access your course from anywhere in the world, earning passive income at the click of a button.

You may choose to sell your online courses through your own blog through email marketing or through Udemy. Udemy is an online learning marketplace that brings together teachers and students. The platform allows teachers to make their courses available to students all across the world and is somewhat similar to Amazon and books. The only difference that instead of selling books, Udemy allows you to sell online courses. Experts on any subject can sell their courses through Udemy. The subject of your course may be anything that you choose to teach from gardening to personal development. Whatever your passion and area of expertise, you can offer a course through Udemy. When your courses sell, you make passive income!

Revenue Sharing

There are some websites that will not only pay you to write articles for them, but who will also pay you a bonus depending on the amount of traffic that your articles generate. This is pay for performance. So if you are good at writing articles that attract lots of interest, this type of model gives you the potential to earn lots of income. However, this model only works if you are able to write for websites that already generate lots and lots of traffic. In addition, the most promising revenue sharing websites are those whose audience is highly engaged and who have good reputations such as Forbes magazine. In addition, the best programs are those that allow you to post as many or as few articles per month as you desire to. And they must offer a base pay as well. Ideally, you want to partner with companies that pay based on traffic rather than based on how many ads are clicked. If you have a knack for creating great headlines and are not afraid to approach big websites, revenue sharing may prove to be a very lucrative source of income for you as a freelance writer.

To truly become rich from writing, you need to have a good mix of both active and passive income. If you want to be truly financially free as a freelance writer, passive income is a must.

PITCHING TIPS

Every freelance writer will get to the point where they are required to pitch to potential clients. Many find the idea of pitching intimidating but it is a skill that must be mastered if you hope to make a living from your writing. A pitch is simply a mini proposal to a potential client in which the freelance writer takes the opportunity to introduce themselves and their services in an appealing way. Your freelance writing career will not take off unless you learn to master the art of pitching. There are simply no two ways about it. It is part and parcel of being a freelance writer so the sooner you get over your fears, the better. And the best way to get over your fear is to do the very thing that you fear doing.

But before you do so, I will be arming you with some tips and advice that will make the process less intimidating and easier for you. I must admit that when I started out in my freelance writing career, I too was fearful of pitching. But I was determined to succeed as a freelance writer and since I had to do something in order to earn, I took the bulls by the horn and started pitching. Those early days were scary but over time, pitching has become like second nature to me. It can become second nature to you as well but you must start by actually pitching to prospective clients.

Where to Find Potential Clients

If you are a new freelance writer, the best place to find clients may be through online freelance writing platforms. These platforms and job boards usually have several jobs listed by clients who are looking for writers. However, if you want to find jobs that are not necessarily listed on job boards, you may need to do some pitching which involves you sending out query letters.

One of the advantages of sending unsolicited queries for unlisted writing opportunities, is that you are likely to find better paying clients. One of the easiest ways to find these clients is through Google searches. The simplest way is to simply type in the keywords "Write for us" into Google search. You should click on the settings button (the gear icon in the top right hand corner) and select advanced search as seen here:

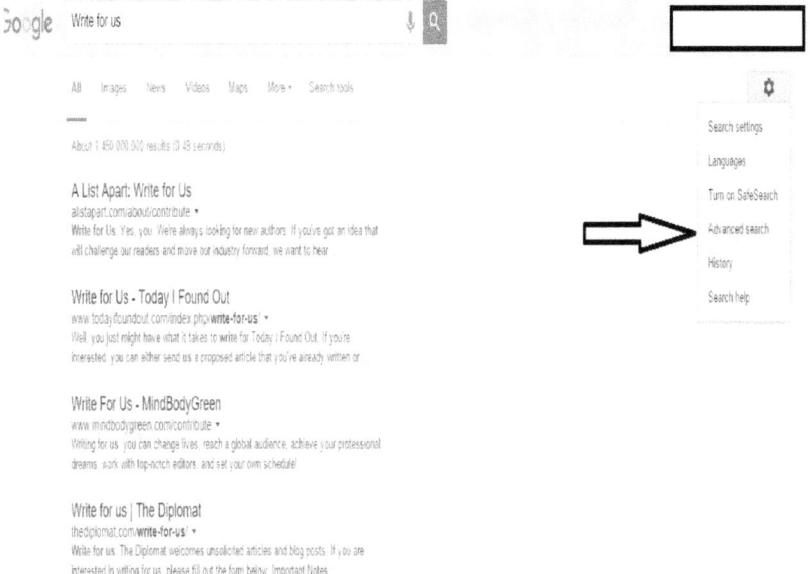

Once you are on the Advanced Search screen, you should enter more specific information to narrow down your search. For example, if your area of expertise is fitness, you can type the word "fitness" where it says "any of the words", click on advanced search and you should end up with a list of websites that need freelance writers in the fitness niche. You can even narrow the search down further by region, or language etc.

Advanced Search

Find pages with...		To do this in the search box.
all these words	Write for us	Type the important words: tri-colour rat terrier
this exact word or phrase		Put exact words in quotes: "rat terrier"
any of these words	fitness	Type OR between all the words you want: miniature OR standard
none of these words		Put a minus sign just before words that you don't want: -rodent, -"Jack Russell"
numbers ranging from	to	Put two full stops between the numbers and add a unit of measurement: 10..35 kg, £300..£500, 2010..2011

Then narrow your results by...

language	any language	▼	Find pages in the language that you select.
region	any region	▼	Find pages published in a particular region.
last update	anytime	▼	Find pages updated within the time that you specify.
site or domain			Search one site (like wikipedia.org) or limit your results to a domain like .edu, .org or .gov
terms appearing	anywhere in the page	▼	Search for terms in the whole page, page title or web address, or links to the page you're looking for.

Here is what your results page would look like:

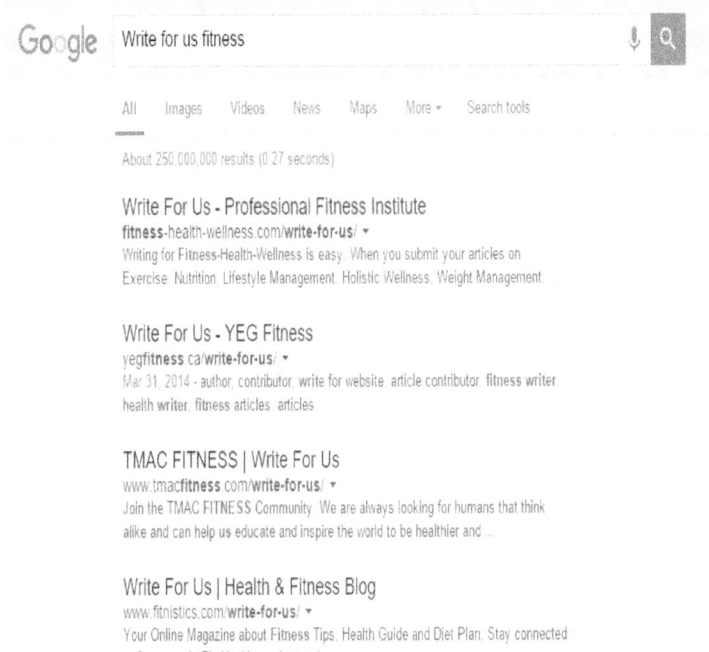

Notice that this search return about 250,000 results. This should be more than enough for you to get started. Begin by reading the descriptions and selecting those that most closely fit the profile of your desired target client. You should go through the list and select a number of these websites that seem like good fits. Next you want to conduct some in depth research on those websites that look like good prospects.

Before you even begin to pitch to a potential client, you must do your homework. You must do some research to find out all you can about your potential client and what type of content they need. You should read their "About" page to get a clear idea of what their website is about. Also, take a look at the content that has already been published on their site to get an idea of their preferred writing style, the average length of their articles, and what topics have already been covered in previous articles. Try to get a feel for who their target audience is and also to note the topics that they have already covered. You don't want to pitch articles that have already been covered by that website.

Make certain that you read all their submission guidelines and that you follow their instructions whenever you submit your pitch or query letter. If they request that you use a specific channel for submission such as via email, ensure that you abide by those instructions. If they request that you use a particular subject in your email, be sure to abide by that also.

Note the names of persons to whom your pitch should be directed and use the person's name whenever you actually write your pitch. It is best to use both first and last name if you are uncertain what the acceptable protocol is. Assuming that you are making submissions via email, your subject line is of utmost importance and will determine whether your submission is given due consideration. The subject line should capture attention and should allow you to stand out among other freelancers. Experts agree that the best subject lines include the content title and the type of article eg. 10 Ways to Get Rid of Cellulite Without Exercising: (Blog Post). Another alternative would be to actually use the editor's name within the subject line which personalizes it and increases the chances of the email being opened. Note that you should be pitching a specific topic, and not just making a general query. That is a recipe for rejection.

Try to keep your pitches as short as possible without leaving out essential details. Remember that there are usually several other pitches that the editor may need to read and you don't want to turn him/her off with an unnecessarily long pitch.

The first paragraph should be a brief introduction of yourself telling the editor why you are a great fit for their website. If you are responding to a posted job, emphasize the skills that the client asked for in their advertisement. Any connection that you can make with the editor is good as well. For example, I once landed a writing gig with a client whose company I had worked with on a part-time basis several years previously. I believe that mentioning this fact gave me the edge over other candidates. Whatever you may have in common with the editor, be sure to mention it, but only if it will improve your chances of landing the gig of course. If you have written for other publications or have your own blog, it may be a good idea to mention these facts briefly especially if you have written for well-known clients. Highlight all relevant accomplishments that you have under your belt.

In the next paragraph, you should flesh out your idea in a little more detail. Give bullet points of the most important subjects that you will cover in your article without going into too much details. Just say enough to arouse the editor's interest. If the editor makes a special request for several topic ideas, be certain to follow suit.

The final paragraph should be used to thank the editor for his/her consideration and to convey your excitement regarding the opportunity. Let him/her know that you hope to hear from them soon. Don't forget to include a copy of your updated resume and a short bio with a link to your blog (if you have one). Some clients do not accept attachments so you may need to include everything in the body of your email. Also, you should include a professional headshot along with your bio.

It goes without saying that your pitch should be free from all grammatical errors and mistakes in spelling or formatting. After all, you are a professional writer. Remember that pitching is similar to sending out a job application and should be given equal importance. It is usually the first impression that a potential client gets of you and you should work hard to make it unforgettable.

FINDING JOBS ON JOB BOARDS AND ONLINE MARKETPLACES

Every freelance writer will get to the point where they are required to pitch to potential clients. Many find the idea of pitching intimidating but it is a skill that must be mastered if you hope to make a living from your writing. A pitch is simply a mini proposal to a potential client in which the freelance writer takes the opportunity to introduce themselves and their services in an appealing way. Your freelance writing career will not take off unless you learn to master the art of pitching. There are simply no two ways about it. It is part and parcel of being a freelance writer so the sooner you get over your fears, the better. And the best way to get over your fear is to do the very thing that you fear doing.

But before you do so, I will be arming you with some tips and advice that will make the process less intimidating and easier for you. I must admit that when I started out in my freelance writing career, I too was fearful of pitching. But I was determined to succeed as a freelance writer and since I had to do something in order to earn, I took the bulls by the horn and started pitching. Those early days were scary but over time, pitching has become like second nature to me. It can become second nature to you as well but you must start by actually pitching to prospective clients.

Where to Find Potential Clients

If you are a new freelance writer, the best place to find clients may be through online freelance writing platforms. These platforms and job boards usually have several jobs listed by clients who are looking for writers. However, if you want to find jobs that are not necessarily listed on job boards, you may need to do some pitching which involves you sending out query letters.

One of the advantages of sending unsolicited queries for unlisted writing opportunities, is that you are likely to find better paying clients. One of the easiest ways to find these clients is through Google searches. The simplest way is to simply type in the keywords "Write for us" into Google search. You should click on the settings button (the gear icon in the top right hand corner) and select advanced search as seen here:

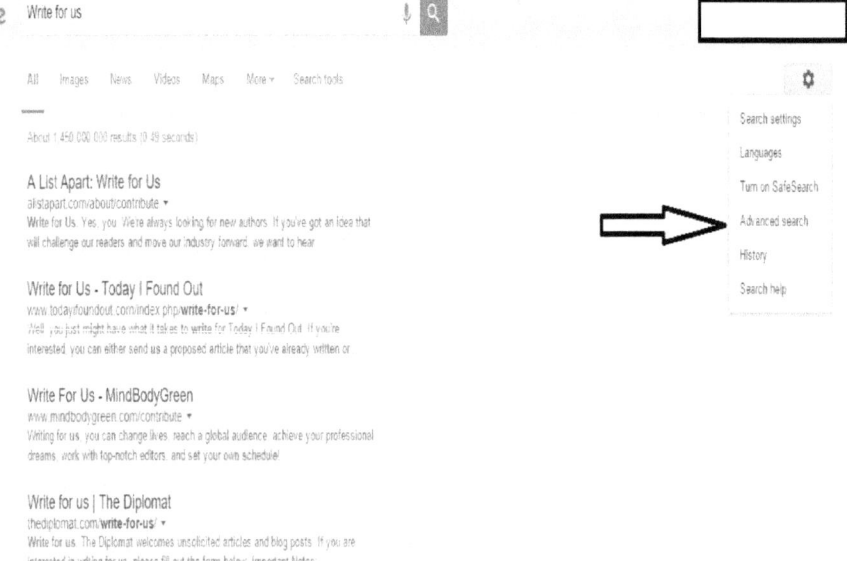

Once you are on the Advanced Search screen, you should enter more specific information to narrow down your search. For example, if your area of expertise is fitness, you can type the word "fitness" where it says "any of the words", click on advanced search and you should end up with a list of websites that need freelance writers in the fitness niche. You can even narrow the search down further by region, or language etc.

Advanced Search

Find pages with...		To do this in the search box.
all these words:	Write for us	Type the important words: tri-colour rat terrier
this exact word or phrase:		Put exact words in quotes: "rat terrier"
any of these words:	fitness	Type OR between all the words you want: miniature OR standard
none of these words:		Put a minus sign just before words that you don't want: -rodent, -"Jack Russell"
numbers ranging from:	to	Put two full stops between the numbers and add a unit of measurement: 10..35 kg, £300..£500, 2010..2011

Then narrow your results by...

language	any language	Find pages in the language that you select
region:	any region	Find pages published in a particular region
last update	anytime	Find pages updated within the time that you specify.
site or domain:		Search one site (like wikipedia.org) or limit your results to a domain like .edu .org or .gov
terms appearing:	anywhere in the page	Search for terms in the whole page, page title or web address, or links to the page you're looking for.

Here is what your results page would look like:

> **Go**ogle Write for us fitness
>
> All   Images   Videos   News   Maps   More ▾   Search tools
>
> About 250,000,000 results (0.27 seconds)
>
> **Write For Us - Professional Fitness Institute**
> **fitness**-health-wellness.com/**write-for-us**/ ▾
> Writing for Fitness-Health-Wellness is easy. When you submit your articles on
> Exercise, Nutrition, Lifestyle Management, Holistic Wellness, Weight Management, ...
>
> **Write For Us - YEG Fitness**
> yeg**fitness**.ca/**write-for-us**/ ▾
> Mar 31, 2014 - author, contributor, write for website, article contributor, fitness writer,
> health writer, fitness articles, articles
>
> **TMAC FITNESS | Write For Us**
> www.tmac**fitness**.com/**write-for-us**/ ▾
> Join the TMAC FITNESS Community. We are always looking for humans that think
> alike and can help us educate and inspire the world to be healthier and ...
>
> **Write For Us | Health & Fitness Blog**
> www.fitnistics.com/**write-for-us**/ ▾
> Your Online Magazine about Fitness Tips, Health Guide and Diet Plan, Stay connected
> to Stay remain Fit, Healthy and attractive.

Notice that this search return about 250,000 results. This should be more than enough for you to get started. Begin by reading the descriptions and selecting those that most closely fit the profile of your desired target client. You should go through the list and select a number of these websites that seem like good fits. Next you want to conduct some in depth research on those websites that look like good prospects.

Before you even begin to pitch to a potential client, you must do your homework. You must do some research to find out all you can about your potential client and what type of content they need. You should read their "About" page to get a clear idea of what their website is about. Also, take a look at the content that has already been published on their site to get an idea of their preferred writing style, the average length of their articles, and what topics have already been covered in previous articles. Try to get a feel for who their target audience is and also to note the topics that they have already covered. You don't want to pitch articles that have already been covered by that website.

Make certain that you read all their submission guidelines and that you follow their instructions whenever you submit your pitch or query letter. If they request that you use a specific channel for submission such as via email, ensure that you abide by those instructions. If they request that you use a particular subject in your email, be sure to abide by that also.

Note the names of persons to whom your pitch should be directed and use the person's name whenever you actually write your pitch. It is best to use both first and last name if you are uncertain what the acceptable protocol is. Assuming that you are making submissions via email, your subject line is of utmost importance and will determine whether your submission is given due consideration. The subject line should capture attention and should allow you to stand out among other freelancers. Experts agree that the best subject lines include the content title and the type of article eg. 10 Ways to Get Rid of Cellulite Without Exercising: (Blog Post). Another alternative would be to actually use the editor's name within the subject line which personalizes it and increases the chances of the email being opened. Note that you should be pitching a specific topic, and not just making a general query. That is a recipe for rejection.

Try to keep your pitches as short as possible without leaving out essential details. Remember that there are usually several other pitches that the editor may need to read and you don't want to turn him/her off with an unnecessarily long pitch.

The first paragraph should be a brief introduction of yourself telling the editor why you are a great fit for their website. If you are responding to a posted job, emphasize the skills that the client asked for in their advertisement. Any connection that you can make with the editor is good as well. For example, I once landed a writing gig with a client whose company I had worked with on a part-time basis several years previously. I believe that mentioning this fact gave me the edge over other candidates. Whatever you may have in common with the editor, be sure to mention it, but only if it will improve your chances of landing the gig of course. If you have written for other publications or have your own blog, it may be a good idea to mention these facts briefly especially if you have written for well-known clients. Highlight all relevant accomplishments that you have under your belt.

In the next paragraph, you should flesh out your idea in a little more detail. Give bullet points of the most important subjects that you will cover in your article without going into too much details. Just say enough to arouse the editor's interest. If the editor makes a special request for several topic ideas, be certain to follow suit.

The final paragraph should be used to thank the editor for his/her consideration and to convey your excitement regarding the opportunity. Let him/her know that you hope to hear from them soon. Don't forget to include a copy of your updated resume and a short bio with a link to your blog (if you have one). Some clients do not accept attachments so you may need to include everything in the body of your email. Also, you should include a professional headshot along with your bio.

It goes without saying that your pitch should be free from all grammatical errors and mistakes in spelling or formatting. After all, you are a professional writer. Remember that pitching is similar to sending out a job application and should be given equal importance. It is usually the first impression that a potential client gets of you and you should work hard to make it unforgettable.

20 FREELANCE WRITING JOB SITES

Here is a list of 20 online marketplaces and job boards that feature several jobs for freelance writers. The pay schedule is also indicated:

1. Guru.com - Pays as soon as employer pays
2. ProBlogger Job Board – Decided with client
3. BloggingPro Job Board – Decided with client
4. Upwork – Two (2) weeks after pay period for hourly jobs, fixed jobs paid on completion of job
5. Freelancer – Twice Weekly
6. Freelance Writing Gigs – Decided with client
7. BloggerJobs.Biz – Decided with client
8. Freelanced – Decided with client
9. Contena – Decided with client
10. Indeed – Decided with client
11. SimplyHired – Decided with client
12. LinkedIn – Decided with client
13. All Indie Writers – Decided with client
14. Paid to Blog – Decided with client
15. Writing Jobz – Every two (2) weeks
16. Constant Content – At the beginning of each month
17. Wizard Writers – Once monthly

18. Writer Bay – Once Monthly
19. Triond – Once monthly
20. The Write Life Job Board – Decided with client

HOW TO AVOID GETTING BAD REVIEWS ON ONLINE MARKETPLACES

There is nothing worse than getting a 1-star review on a freelance writing platform. While not every client will love your work each and every time, there are steps that you can take to reduce the chances of getting bad reviews on freelance writing websites. Obviously, if you consistently produce poor quality work, bad reviews are bound to come. But since no freelance writer wants a bad online reputation, I will share with you some ways that you can avoid getting the dreaded 1-star or 2-star review.

Spell it Out - Freelance writers should never be shy about letting prospects know that they are willing to put in their best efforts on any job and that they expect a good review. While you can't demand a glowing review, use your description to inform prospects that you are willing to work with them until they are satisfied with your work. However, I would suggest limiting the number of revisions that you offer to 3. Never offer unlimited reviews.

Say it Loud - As soon as you are awarded a job, you should use the opportunity to send your new client a message thanking them for contracting your services. Since not many freelance writers bother to do this, it will make you stand out as an exceptional freelance writer. Also use this opportunity to ask your client to clarify anything that you may not be 100% certain of concerning their order. This will avoid any misunderstanding leading into the relationship. Tell them when to expect delivery of your order and try your best to deliver sooner than promised.

Time the job properly - Accurately estimating how long each job will take to complete is essential to maintaining a good relationship with your clients. Even if you can reasonably deliver the job in 24 hours, give yourself an extra day just in case something comes up and you can't deliver as agreed. So instead of promising to deliver in 24 hours, promise to deliver in 48 hours. However, you should still aim to deliver that order within 24 hours. This will definitely delight your client. Nevertheless, be careful not to rush the order so much that the quality is compromised.

Communication is Key - In any relationship communication is key. Whenever you establish a relationship with a client, ensure that the communication is excellent on your side. If for example, you can't deliver an order in time, be sure to inform the client way ahead of time. Let them know what challenges you are facing and when they can expect the order to be submitted. Most clients will appreciate this even if their order is slightly delayed. Just ensure that your clients are informed at all times about the status of their order. Also, if you are experiencing problems fulfilling an order, let the client know about it. It makes no sense keeping it to yourself and delaying the order. You just may end up with a bad review.

Under promise and over deliver - Promise less than you can deliver and then deliver more than you promised. This is the key to establishing a good, long-lasting relationship with your clients. Like in any other service business, you should always aim to go above and beyond what the ordinary freelance writer will deliver.

Seal the Deal - When you have completed the client's order, send them a message along with the order. Thank them again for their business and ask them to let you know if they are not 100% satisfied with the job that you have done. If they do point out an area that they are not totally satisfied with, quickly correct the problem and resubmit the order. Let the client know that you look forward to working with them again.

If you follow these steps, you will avoid getting bad reviews and attract more 5 star and 4 star reviews. In addition, you will attract repeat clients.

REASONS WHY EVERY FREELANCE WRITER SHOULD START A BLOG

If you are a freelance writer who is contemplating whether you should start a blog or not, you need to read this right now. As a freelance writer myself, my freelance writing career has benefited tremendously simply by the fact that I decided to start a blog and to maintain it. I would like to share with you 5 compelling reasons why you need to start a blog, and why the sooner you do so, the better.

1. To Create a More Professional Brand Image – As a freelance writer, you are the brand, you are the brand image. It is very difficult to build a brand image online without a blog. Yes, there is social media but social media followers can be fickle.

In your quest to make an income from freelance writing, it is important that you portray a professional image. When you start a blog, the message that it sends out is "I am a professional freelance writer".

I have seen freelance writers with Twitter profiles with no blog link and the first thing that I think to myself is "Okay, where is your blog?" Where can I find out more about you? Where can I go to see some of your work? Because the truth is, if you are really serious about earning a good income from freelance writing, you need your very own space on the internet; you need to start a blog.

Think about it like this. Put yourself in the shoes of a prospective client. If there are 2 freelance writers who are equally qualified and talented and both are vying for the same client, but the other freelance writer has a blog and you don't, who do you think is more likely to get the offer? If you guessed the freelance writer with the blog, then you guessed correctly.

Because really and truly, in a sense, having a blog is similar to registering your business. Businesses that are registered tend to be more trusted than those that aren't and clients feel more comfortable doing business with someone who appears to be serious about doing business.

Likewise, if you start a blog, it indicates that you are a serious and professional freelance writer. You don't want to give the impression that you have no abiding city. Prospects need to know that they can find you online, if they need to find you. Social media is for socializing. A blog is where you conduct business.

2. Start a Blog to Get More Leads – As a freelance writer, when you start a blog, you give yourself the opportunity to be found by people who are searching online for the services that you offer. Do you know how huge that opportunity is and what it can mean for you in dollars and cents?

Just simply having a blog gives you the opportunity to show up in search engine result pages (SERPs) and increases your chances of making sales. Did you know that over 100 billion searches are conducted on Google alone each month and that 1.17 billion people search Google every month for things that they may want to purchase? You can't benefit from this type of traffic if you don't start a blog.

Just a side note. I don't want you to confuse a blog with a website. Every blog is a website but not every website is a blog. A blog is where dynamic content is created. This is what drives traffic. This is what says to Google, "what I am saying is relevant, it is up to date and it is current". A website on the other hand is more static and changes rarely.

This is why every website should have a blog section where up-to-date, relevant information is fed to the search engines on a regular basis. The blog is what is going to send more leads to you as a freelance writer. Isn't this alone sufficient reason for you to start a blog? If you still need convincing, read on.

3. To Build Authority and Brand Awareness – If you do your investigations, you will realize that the most financially successfully freelance writers have their own blog. In addition, if you should question them, you would learn that having a blog has been the main contributing factor to their success. The blog is the tool that they use for marketing and to build authority and brand awareness in their specific niches.

When you start a blog, after a while you will realize that you have created a vast database of knowledge that helps to portray you as an authority in your niche. Can you imagine having hundreds of articles in a single location about a particular subject? This database is a valuable resource that tells people that you know your stuff and that you are a leader in your field. The more blog posts or articles that you put out, the more people become aware of you and your services. This is how you build authority and brand awareness online.

4. To Increase Your Influence – If you start a blog as a freelance writer, you are immediately increasing your influence. A blog is what is going to give you an audible voice online and it is what you will use to influence people's decisions. By simply using blogging as a means of voicing your opinion on a matter or by giving people additional information on a subject, you are influencing their views and giving them different perspectives.

People listen to bloggers. This is why some companies are willing to pay bloggers to use their products and to write product reviews on their behalf. A person of influence will find it easier to attract sales than someone who has very little influence. Blogging gives you the avenue to connect with people emotionally which is really what drives sales. As a freelance writer, this is what you want to do, drive sales.

5. To Improve Your Writing Skills – One sure way of becoming a better writer, is by writing more often. Blogging is all about writing and researching. Once you start a blog, you will be writing more often. This means that you have the opportunity to increase your writing speed, increase your knowledge since you will have to conduct research for your writing, and to get your creative juices flowing freely on a regular basis.

Since I decided to start a blog, my writing speed has increased tremendously and I can now easily write 3000 words on a daily basis. As a freelance writer, this means that I can complete more jobs on a daily basis and therefore earn more. The same thing applies to you.

Influence is the ability to connect, engage and get individuals to act on what you have to say. Influence is increasing your listener's trust, and believability in you" – Stacey Hanke
While blogging does take time and effort, the costs of blogging outweigh the benefits to you as a freelance writer. At the end of the day, if you make the decision to start a blog, you will appear more professional, get more leads, build authority and brand awareness, increase your influence and also improve your writing skills. Why not start a blog today? It's easier than you may think!

MARKETING AND BRAND AWARENESS FOR FREELANCE WRITERS

What will set you apart as a freelance writer who can be classified as rich, is not necessarily your ability to write well, but your ability to effectively market yourself and your services. Just as with best-selling authors, it is not necessarily the best writers who become best sellers. It is those who get the marketing right – whether they do it themselves or they hire someone to market on their behalf.

As a Freelance Writer who wants to earn money online, it is important that you establish and maintain marketing campaigns and campaigns to build and establish brand awareness. The best way to do this online is through social media marketing and blogging. This means that you need to establish social media profiles on different social media platforms. The previous chapter already details the benefits of maintaining a blog as a freelance writer. In this chapter, we will discuss how to make the most of social media in branding yourself and getting your services in front of potential customers

There is no hard and fast rule about which social media platforms you should use. In fact, it depends greatly on which social media platforms your target customers use more regularly. It may take a little trial and error to determine which platforms are the best platforms to use to facilitate your social media marketing efforts. Regardless of which social media platforms you choose to use, there are a few things that you need to bear in mind:

Maintain Separate Personal and Professional Social Media Accounts

Ideally, you should maintain separate social media accounts for your personal socializing and your freelance writing business. This way, you can maintain your professionalism on your business social media accounts. You don't want to be having conversations with your friends on the same platform that you are conducting business on. As the saying goes, business and pleasure don't mix very well.

This is especially applicable to your Facebook account. You must create a Facebook fan page that is separate and apart from your personal profile. While you can invite your Facebook friends to like your Facebook fan page and to follow you there, do not be tempted to use your personal account to market your freelance writing services. People tend to get turned off when their newsfeeds are filled with promotional posts on a platform that is supposed to be for socializing. Don't run the risk of your friends avoiding you or unfriending you simply because you are filling their newsfeeds with what may be regarded as spam. Furthermore, if you do not yet know, let me tell you something that you need to bear in mind as you launch or grow your freelance writing career. Do not rely on friends or family to be the biggest supporters of your freelance writing business. You will be greatly disappointed if you do. I speak from experience when I say this. And it's just not my own experience. This has been the experience of many freelance writers. Build your professional following separate and apart from your friendships.

Always build a professional image on your professional social media accounts. This means that your profile pictures, your cover images, the images that you upload and share, the messages that you post, everything should look and feel professional. If you are building a career as a professional freelance writer, it means that your social media updates should also be free from careless grammatical errors and spelling mistakes. While it may be okay to use "internet slang" or "internet language" such as "lol" or "smh", try to avoid using these as much as possible on your professional social media profiles. It is much better to err on the side of caution than to let down your guard and have it backfire or blow up in your face.

Although you need to maintain professionalism, it is okay to show your real self and to show bits and pieces of who you are on a personal level. So you can sometimes share some photos of you enjoying yourself somewhere or doing something fun. Just don't overdo it and don't be tempted to share information that is overly personal with your followers. It can be sometimes difficult to strike the balance between being professional and being human and friendly but you should err on the side of caution rather than being guilty of sharing too much personal information on social media.

Although you are the only one who can decide which social media networks you will use to establish your freelance writing career, there is one social media platform that I highly recommend for all freelance writers – LinkedIn. I have found LinkedIn to be a great source of business and customers for me simply by maintaining a LinkedIn profile. I did not deliberately seek out any freelance writing opportunities on LinkedIn but I have been contacted on several occasions by persons who saw my profile on LinkedIn and who wanted to access my services. The LinkedIn platform is a very good marketing tool that is ideal for freelance writers to showcase their writing talents online. If you don't maintain your own blog, you should certainly consider using LinkedIn Pulse as a blogging platform that will give you well needed exposure. And if you do have a blog, you don't need to worry about having to post on your own blog then having to find new content to post on LinkedIn. Because the truth is that you can syndicate your blog posts on LinkedIn and benefit from the increased traffic and exposure that the platform can afford you.

Consistency is the key to Social Media Marketing Success

As a professional freelance writer, it is very important that you remain consistent with your social media marketing efforts. Updating and making posts to your social media accounts only when you feel like it is a recipe for failure. It is very important that you post regularly to any of the social media accounts that you maintain. This is the very best way to build brand awareness and to keep your products and services at the forefront of prospects' minds whenever they have to make a purchase decision. If they hardly see you or hear from you, they will very likely not purchase from you. Get this one thing straight.

"People buy from those they know, like and trust."

It's as simple as that. If people don't know anything about you, they are unlikely to buy from you. And the only way that they can get to know you better online is through what you share with them, what you say to them, and how you relate to and interact with them on social media platforms.

There is one particular marketer who I follow on Twitter who I admire tremendously. She has a specific product that she markets through Twitter consistently. I knew nothing about this person before seeing her tweets on Twitter but she is so consistent in her marketing that if the product that she markets was not so expensive, I would definitely purchase from her even though I don't know her personally. But her consistency alone tells me that she is committed, dedicated, believes in what she is marketing and can be found if the need arises. And that's the message that you want to send to your social media followers. If your followers hardly see you, they won't get the opportunity to get to know you, like you or to trust you.

It can be very difficult to find the time to consistently post to several different social media accounts on a regular basis. This is why professional freelance writers and other professionals depend on social media marketing tools such as Hootsuite to do the heavy lifting on their behalf. Hootsuite is a tool that you can use to schedule your social media marketing messages for publishing. You can schedule and publish up to 350 posts on up to 50 different social media profiles using Hootsuite. This tool has been an invaluable time-saver for me as I grow my freelance writing career. It gives me time to focus on my writing while ensuring that my social media marketing is still up to date and up to standard. If you plan to run your freelance writing business professionally, you should seriously consider using Hootsuite to schedule your social media updates.

However, one word of caution. Be certain that you are not only posting messages on social media without interacting with your social media followers. The worst thing you can do is to flood your fans or followers with your messages but fail to be human and to interact with them one on one. As a freelance writer, you must take the time to talk back to your fans, to comment on what they have shared, to like their posts, to re-share valuable content and to just build great and lasting online relationships. Because even though it is social media, it is relationship building. Relationship building is essential to every type of business undertaking and freelance writing is no different.

I must admit that I am not the best at this but I am getting better at it. I am really making a conscious effort to interact more online because that is how relationships are established. It is not through one-way link dumping. It is through conversations and interactions. If you take a look at those persons who do well on social media, you will realize that they interact a lot with their followers. They give shout outs, they mention others, they make comments and they just make an effort to be truly social. You should follow suite in your attempt to build a following on social media.

One additional perk that consistency on social media offers, is that it allows you to grow your organic following easily and effortlessly. The more you follow others and interact with them, the more likely they are to follow you back. There are some persons who "buy" followers but I strongly advise against this practice if you want to really succeed as a freelance writer. This is because followers that are bought are usually not human, but are actually robots, and even if they are human, chances are they are not your ideal target audience. Therefore, the chance of them purchasing any of your products or services or even building a meaningful relationship with you is slim. It is much better to build your following organically with the opportunity to connect with people who can make a positive difference to your career.

HOW TO LAND MORE FREELANCE WRITER JOBS

What will set you apart as a freelance writer who can be classified as rich, is not necessarily your ability to write well, but your ability to effectively market yourself and your services. Just as with best-selling authors, it is not necessarily the best writers who become best sellers. It is those who get the marketing right – whether they do it themselves or they hire someone to market on their behalf.

As a Freelance Writer who wants to earn money online, it is important that you establish and maintain marketing campaigns and campaigns to build and establish brand awareness. The best way to do this online is through social media marketing and blogging. This means that you need to establish social media profiles on different social media platforms. The previous chapter already details the benefits of maintaining a blog as a freelance writer. In this chapter, we will discuss how to make the most of social media in branding yourself and getting your services in front of potential customers

There is no hard and fast rule about which social media platforms you should use. In fact, it depends greatly on which social media platforms your target customers use more regularly. It may take a little trial and error to determine which platforms are the best platforms to use to facilitate your social media marketing efforts. Regardless of which social media platforms you choose to use, there are a few things that you need to bear in mind:

Maintain Separate Personal and Professional Social Media Accounts

Ideally, you should maintain separate social media accounts for your personal socializing and your freelance writing business. This way, you can maintain your professionalism on your business social media accounts. You don't want to be having conversations with your friends on the same platform that you are conducting business on. As the saying goes, business and pleasure don't mix very well.

This is especially applicable to your Facebook account. You must create a Facebook fan page that is separate and apart from your personal profile. While you can invite your Facebook friends to like your Facebook fan page and to follow you there, do not be tempted to use your personal account to market your freelance writing services. People tend to get turned off when their newsfeeds are filled with promotional posts on a platform that is supposed to be for socializing. Don't run the risk of your friends avoiding you or unfriending you simply because you are filling their newsfeeds with what may be regarded as spam. Furthermore, if you do not yet know, let me tell you something that you need to bear in mind as you launch or grow your freelance writing career. Do not rely on friends or family to be the biggest supporters of your freelance writing business. You will be greatly disappointed if you do. I speak from experience when I say this. And it's just not my own experience. This has been the experience of many freelance writers. Build your professional following separate and apart from your friendships.

Always build a professional image on your professional social media accounts. This means that your profile pictures, your cover images, the images that you upload and share, the messages that you post, everything should look and feel professional. If you are building a career as a professional freelance writer, it means that your social media updates should also be free from careless grammatical errors and spelling mistakes. While it may be okay to use "internet slang" or "internet language" such as "lol" or "smh", try to avoid using these as much as possible on your professional social media profiles. It is much better to err on the side of caution than to let down your guard and have it backfire or blow up in your face.

Although you need to maintain professionalism, it is okay to show your real self and to show bits and pieces of who you are on a personal level. So you can sometimes share some photos of you enjoying yourself somewhere or doing something fun. Just don't overdo it and don't be tempted to share information that is overly personal with your followers. It can be sometimes difficult to strike the balance between being professional and being human and friendly but you should err on the side of caution rather than being guilty of sharing too much personal information on social media.

Although you are the only one who can decide which social media networks you will use to establish your freelance writing career, there is one social media platform that I highly recommend for all freelance writers – LinkedIn. I have found LinkedIn to be a great source of business and customers for me simply by maintaining a LinkedIn profile. I did not deliberately seek out any freelance writing opportunities on LinkedIn but I have been contacted on several occasions by persons who saw my profile on LinkedIn and who wanted to access my services. The LinkedIn platform is a very good marketing tool that is ideal for freelance writers to showcase their writing talents online. If you don't maintain your own blog, you should certainly consider using LinkedIn Pulse as a blogging platform that will give you well needed exposure. And if you do have a blog, you don't need to worry about having to post on your own blog then having to find new content to post on LinkedIn. Because the truth is that you can syndicate your blog posts on LinkedIn and benefit from the increased traffic and exposure that the platform can afford you.

Consistency is the key to Social Media Marketing Success
As a professional freelance writer, it is very important that you remain consistent with your social media marketing efforts. Updating and making posts to your social media accounts only when you feel like it is a recipe for failure. It is very important that you post regularly to any of the social media accounts that you maintain. This is the very best way to build brand awareness and to keep your products and services at the forefront of prospects' minds whenever they have to make a purchase decision. If they hardly see you or hear from you, they will very likely not purchase from you. Get this one thing straight.
"People buy from those they know, like and trust."
It's as simple as that. If people don't know anything about you, they are unlikely to buy from you. And the only way that they can get to know you better online is through what you share with them, what you say to them, and how you relate to and interact with them on social media platforms.
There is one particular marketer who I follow on Twitter who I admire tremendously. She has a specific product that she markets through Twitter consistently. I knew nothing about this person before seeing her tweets on Twitter but she is so consistent in her marketing that if the product that she markets was not so expensive, I would definitely purchase from her even though I don't know her personally. But her consistency alone tells me that she is committed, dedicated, believes in what she is marketing and can be found if the need arises. And that's the message that you want to send to your social media followers. If your followers hardly see you, they won't get the opportunity to get to know you, like you or to trust you.
It can be very difficult to find the time to consistently post to several different social media accounts on a regular basis. This is why professional freelance writers and other professionals depend on social media marketing tools such as Hootsuite to do the heavy lifting on their behalf. Hootsuite is a tool that you can use to schedule your social media marketing messages for publishing. You can schedule and publish up to 350 posts on up to 50 different social media profiles using Hootsuite. This tool has been an invaluable time-saver for me as I grow my freelance writing career. It gives

me time to focus on my writing while ensuring that my social media marketing is still up to date and up to standard. If you plan to run your freelance writing business professionally, you should seriously consider using Hootsuite to schedule your social media updates.

However, one word of caution. Be certain that you are not only posting messages on social media without interacting with your social media followers. The worst thing you can do is to flood your fans or followers with your messages but fail to be human and to interact with them one on one. As a freelance writer, you must take the time to talk back to your fans, to comment on what they have shared, to like their posts, to re-share valuable content and to just build great and lasting online relationships. Because even though it is social media, it is relationship building. Relationship building is essential to every type of business undertaking and freelance writing is no different.

I must admit that I am not the best at this but I am getting better at it. I am really making a conscious effort to interact more online because that is how relationships are established. It is not through one-way link dumping. It is through conversations and interactions. If you take a look at those persons who do well on social media, you will realize that they interact a lot with their followers. They give shout outs, they mention others, they make comments and they just make an effort to be truly social. You should follow suite in your attempt to build a following on social media.

One additional perk that consistency on social media offers, is that it allows you to grow your organic following easily and effortlessly. The more you follow others and interact with them, the more likely they are to follow you back. There are some persons who "buy" followers but I strongly advise against this practice if you want to really succeed as a freelance writer. This is because followers that are bought are usually not human, but are actually robots, and even if they are human, chances are they are not your ideal target audience. Therefore, the chance of them purchasing any of your products or services or even building a meaningful relationship with you is slim. It is much better to build your following organically with the opportunity to connect with people who can make a positive difference to your career.

HOW TO GROW YOUR FREELANCE WRITING BUSINESS

Freelance writing is a great career choice. However, there is only so much that one person can write and no more. So how do you actually grow your freelance writing business without having to churn out more content? This is a question that many freelance writers have and I would like to address this issue. I will share 4 ways that you can grow your freelance writing business so that you can earn more as a freelance writer.

Consider Outsourcing – In your freelance writing career, you may get to the point where you have several freelance writing jobs to do but not enough time to get everything done in a timely manner while preserving the quality of your work. Outsourcing minor jobs is an excellent way to free yourself up to work on bigger projects, while still capitalizing on smaller projects.

However, the key to successful outsourcing is finding reliable and talented help. You don't necessarily have to outsource the actual writing of your pieces. For example, you can outsource the research aspect of your writing and pay someone to simply gather the research and to put it together in one document for you. Then you can do the actual writing of the piece yourself.

What outsourcing does is that it frees up some of your time so that you can concentrate on more challenging tasks without having to turn down other jobs because of lack of time. While outsourcing is a good option for growing your freelance writing business, you must ensure that the talent that you recruit is reliable and committed to producing quality work. Selecting the wrong person could jeopardize your reputation so spend some time in the actual selection process.

Re-purpose and Recycle Your Writing – Re-purposing your writing is a great way to grow your freelance writing business. What this means is that you take a piece that you have written and you change something about it so that it can be used in different ways. For example, after writing an article, I can re-purpose that same article by creating a Powerpoint presentation from it and sharing it on Slideshare, or I can create a video based on the same article, or I can use the article as a chapter in a book that I produce, or I can even get the article translated into a different language and earn from it in new markets. All it takes to re-purpose your writing is a little creativity and some "outside-the-box thinking".

By re-purposing your writing, you can earn from your freelance writing efforts several times over from the same information presented in a different way. So let's say that I write an article and publish it on Hubpages or on my own blog and that I earn a commission when people make purchases of items that I mention or link to in my articles. I can take that same article and produce a Youtube video which could lead to further sales of products, and I can also create a Slideshare presentation and monetize it.

With a little effort, your freelance writing can easily be re-purposed so that you can earn more. While I admit that it can take some time to re-purpose your writing, bear in mind that a single document can help you to earn several times over once it has been re-purposed.

Write An Online Course – The beauty about writing an online course is that you only need to write it once but you can earn from it while you sleep. Thanks to Udemy and other such platforms, you can write a course and market it with Udemy. They receive millions of visitors who are ready to pay for the information that you offer in your courses. As long as you have expertise in an area and have a knack for sharing your knowledge through writing, you can expand your freelance writing business through this means. The more courses you write, the greater your earning potential.

Seek Repeat Business from Clients – Getting a single writing gig is okay but if you really want to grow your freelance writing business, you need to create more sustainable sources of income. One way of doing this is by offering to write on a continuous basis for clients who you have done work for in the past. Consider packaging your writing services and offering it to them in an attractive way.

For example, you may offer a client a discount price per article if they purchase a minimum number of articles from you on a monthly basis. Also, you may offer additional services such as proofreading or editing for them. You may even offer to rewrite their "About" page or to help them to post messages on social media.

It is always easier to get business from a client who you have worked for before than to acquire new clients. So consider calling up or emailing some of your previous clients to generate new interest.

Seek Bigger Clients – More and more corporate organizations are seeking the services of freelancers. These bigger organizations are sometimes better able to compensate you for your freelance writing. By diversifying your client profile, you can grow your freelance writing business.

Freelance writing can be very lucrative. Implement these simple ideas and watch your freelance writing business grow to new levels.

HOW TO DEAL WITH THE FREELANCE WRITING CLIENT FROM HELL

If you are already a freelance writer, you have probably encountered your fair share of freelance writing clients from hell. If you are new, you are likely to encounter at least a few highly disagreeable clients throughout your career. These are those clients who want an arm and a leg but who are willing to pay only a penny or two for your efforts. There is always that one client who asks for endless reviews, always orders at the last minute and always expects to be given top priority. Have you met him/her yet? Keep on freelancing. You are bound to meet him/her eventually. Today, I want to share with you a few strategies for dealing with that freelance writing client from hell.

Firstly, don't take it personally when a client gives you a hard time. It may just be their personality or they may be going through a really bad time and just need to vent. Whatever you do, DO NOT speak down to, curse or get so upset that you say something that you will later regret. It is very important that you keep calm and get to the root of the problem rather than simply assuming that the client is just difficult.

Many of these clients who seem to come straight from hell are steeped in the employer/employee culture and tend to treat freelance writers like employees. They don't realize that a freelance writer is a free agent who may have chosen to enter into a contractual relationship with them. However, this does not give them the right to treat freelance writers as if they are employees who stand the chance of losing their jobs if......(fill in the blanks).

Don't Act Desperate – From the very beginning, as a freelance writer, you must establish yourself as a professional and conduct yourself as such. Resist the urge to be overly grateful and thankful simply because someone has chosen to hire you to complete a job for which you will be paid. Remember that they need you as much as you need them. But don't give them the upper hand from the start by acting desperate.

This includes setting reasonable rates and sticking to them. Do not negotiate your way out of a decent compensation because you want the job. Be grateful, but don't overdo it. A simple thank you is sufficient. As a freelance writer, you should never give a client the impression that they are your only source of income. Even if they are, they don't need to know that! And if they do know, it just gives them more reason to treat you anyway they please. So the ball is in your court from the beginning of the relationship to set the standard of operation.

Be Clear about your Terms – In order to avoid a potential conflict with a client in the first place, you must ensure that your terms are very clear and that the client understands exactly what it is that they will get when they order your service. When I just started out as freelance writer, I lost a great deal of money because I assumed that the client knew what I would be delivering instead of making it clear to them. So I ended up with quite a few cancellations and endless revision requests.

I remember when a client contracted me to provide them with a list of a certain type of company along with brief descriptions for each company. Well, based on the money the client was prepared to spend, I prepared a list of 50 items. I was taken aback when they client proceeded to tell me that I was a rip off and a scam and that she wanted her money back because she expected at least 100 items! 100 items for $x? Was she crazy? In the end, she ended up cancelling the job AND giving me a 1-star review!

Guess who never made that mistake again? As soon as this happened I made steps to clarify exactly what I was offering and exactly what clients should expect for $x or $y. As a new freelance writer, it is easy to be vague and end up losing. If you work on the online forums, this is especially important. As long as you are clear about what you have to offer and what the client should expect, you should be okay.

Ask Questions to Ensure Understanding – Even if you think you understand what the client wants, don't assume. Repeat the client's request back to him or her and ask whether what you understand is the same as what they have requested of you. It is up to you as the freelance writer to make sure that you and your client are speaking the same language and that the understanding is mutual. This is especially important if your client's first language is not English. Go the extra mile to ensure that you understand what they want from you.

Do not offer unlimited revisions – Okay I know that not everyone will agree with me on this. I understand the view that you may want to please the client and so you are willing to go the extra mile to ensure satisfaction. But I think this is just opening yourself up for abuse. If the client knows that they can get unlimited revisions, they may abuse the privilege.

I know of cases where freelance writing clients change their original order after the freelance writer has completed or almost completed the job and expect a smile and a nod when a revision request is made. I know that there will be cases when changes need to be made but unlimited revisions, no, I don't think so! Set a limit. I think 3 revisions are more than adequate and if you can't get it right after 3 revisions, either something is wrong with you or something is wrong with the client.

Do Your Best Work Always – As a freelance writer, you should always give your best to your clients. Do not short change the client in any way. When you have done your best and the client is not satisfied, it means that the client's expectations have not been met. Try to act calmly and rationally and try to address the client's concerns professionally. Sometimes it is a matter of misunderstanding. If you have done your best and have discussed concerns with the client and he/she is still not satisfied, you probably are not the best person for the job. If you find that the client is upset about what you have submitted, I would suggest apologizing and offering a refund. Then just move on.

End the Relationship if Necessary – Sometimes in your freelance writing career, you may simply need to end the relationship with a client. If you find that you can't please him/her then it makes no sense for you to frustrate yourself by taking the relationship any further. A simple misunderstanding is okay but if it begins to happen too often, the relationship needs to end. Don't worry, there are other clients out there who are willing to hire you.

I remember ending a relationship with a client once because I just couldn't please her. At the time she was my biggest client. But I was not prepared to sacrifice my happiness to please her at all costs. It was a scary thing to do but after careful consideration and prayer, I decided it was the right decision to make. God has since opened the door to several bigger, more agreeable clients with whom I get along well. Sometimes, you just need to end the relationship.

Choose Your Clients Carefully – After some time doing freelance writing and working with clients, you will know how to choose your clients. Avoid persons who are unwilling to pay you fairly or who approach you as if you are an employee. Don't allow clients to establish deadlines for you. You set your deadlines based on your schedule and allow the client to decide whether they can work with your schedule or not. If they insist on telling you when you need to do what, they may be better off hiring an employee. Once you agree on a deadline, meet that deadline at all costs. Never let it be said that you don't meet deadlines.

GUEST BLOGGING

One of the best ways to propel your online freelance writing career is through guest blogging. Guest blogging is writing an article for a blogger that will be published on that blogger's blog or website. You may be wondering why anyone would want to publish an article on someone else's blog or website especially if they are not being compensated to do so. I will answer that question shortly. Suffice it to say that guest blogging is usually undertaken as a means of gaining exposure and building brand awareness. Some guest blogging opportunities are paid, but regardless of whether compensation is offered, guest blogging is an excellent way of building your freelance writing business if you are also a blogger.

The most compelling reason to do guest blogging is that guest blogging exposes you to the audience of the blogger for whom you are blogging.

This provides opportunities for you to reach and influence more people with your work. Usually the blogs that you do guest blogs for already have lots of traffic and a well-established audience. Guest blogging puts you in front of that audience. I never understood the benefits of guest blogging until well into my freelance writing career. But I wish someone had told me about it earlier. I would have reached further in my freelance writing career in much less time.

Misconceptions About Freelance Guest Blogging that You Need to Flush

I have not always appreciated or understood the many virtues of guest blogging. All along I have heard that guest blogging is the way to build your blog authority and to create valuable backlinks but I really couldn't fathom how publishing my best work on someone else's website or blog would be beneficial to me. But, I finally got it. I finally understand why guest blogging is so valuable and why every blogger who wants to expand their audience and to increase traffic to their blog should definitely engage in guest blogging. Here are some common misconceptions about guest blogging that you need to get rid of:

1. **Guest Blogging only sends traffic to the host's blog** – Don't laugh but I actually held this belief for a very long time. This was really the main reason why I ignored guest blogging for a very long time. I was of the impression that as a guest blogger, I would prepare some of my best work, only to have it published on some other blogger's website, and send traffic to them instead of to me. I just couldn't understand the logic behind this. But, boy was I oh so very, very wrong. Guest blogging can send the guest blogger tons and tons of traffic as well and at the end of the day it really is a win-win situation where traffic is concerned. When you engage in guest blogging, if your article is good and interesting, readers are going to want to find out more about you. They are going to want to click your gravatar and to visit your blog to find out who the awesome writer is behind the valuable information that you shared as a guest blogger. What does that mean for you? It means traffic, it means exposure to audiences you may never have reached on your own. It means new leads, new readers, new opportunities to get subscribers and new opportunities to make more sales! I was so concerned about what I would be giving away as a guest blogger that I never stopped to think about what I would be getting in return.

2. **Guest Blogging is giving away my services for free** – Technically speaking, when you decide to accept a guest blogging opportunity, you will be giving away your services for free. Because the fact is that many guest blogging opportunities are unpaid opportunities. So what's the sense of spending hours crafting a hit article that will appear on someone else's website only to earn zero dollars and zero cents from your efforts? Let's look at the situation a little closer. Yes, it's true. You will make no money for guest blogging directly. In other words, don't expect to collect a check at the end of the process once your article has been published. But

here is what you can expect. Long term sales. Long term traffic. Long term results! While you may not see the money right away, if you do things the right way, guest blogging can end up being a very lucrative venture for you. In fact, guest blogging can help to catapult your blogging and writing career like you never imagined. Here is how it would work. You spend a few hours crafting a winning article which appears on the website of an influencer who already has tons and tons of traffic to their website. People read your guest post, like it, follow through and find you on your own blog. This could be the open door to several other *paid* writing opportunities. Someone who has read your guest post may like it so much that they offer to pay you to write for them. The possibilities for earning indirectly from guest blogging are endless.

3. **Guest blogging is only helping to further build someone else's influence, not mine** – Remember that if someone allows you to guest blog on their site, they are essentially endorsing you as a writer. This sends the message to readers that this guest blogger knows what he/she is talking about. As a blogger who is competing with every other blogger on the internet for a voice and for traffic, being invited to do guest blogging on an influencer's blog is helping to put you in the spotlight. It is helping to build awareness of your personal brand and awareness about you as a professional. Have you ever visited a blog and seen something like "as appeared on ...." and it goes on to list some of the websites where that blogger's work has appeared? This is what guest blogging allows you to do. To instantly build *your* credibility and *your* influence. It allows you to say, hello world, I am such a great writer that "XYZ Magazine" has chosen to publish my work on their site.

4. **Guest Blogging is not worth my time** – Don't fall for this lie. The time you spend doing guest blogging is likely to pay off several times over if done strategically. Yes, you could spend the time writing your own blog posts for your own blog or writing for pay. But, it is definitely worth it to invest at least some of your time to guest blogging. Because as a blogger, leverage is one of the best ways to grow and expand your career. You use a little of your time to invest in someone else's blog, in order to reap rich rewards in the future on the back end. One little guest post can help you to grow faster, deeper and wider than you could on your own. It's about working smarter, not harder. Guest blogging is free advertising for you! Now if that's not worth your time, I don't know what is!

5. **Guest Blogging is not worth it if the link is no follow** – Some

bloggers will only agree to guest blog if the link that they get is a do follow link. While a do follow link is ideal, don't discount the advantages of a no follow link. So you may not get the advantage of getting a do follow link back to your blog but here are some of the advantages that you will get. A no follow link will still help you to build awareness, it may lead to sales of products from your blog, it may lead to a bookmarking of your site by someone who reads your article, it may open the door to several other opportunities.

So there you have it folks. Let's get rid of the misconceptions about guest blogging and let's go out there and build brand awareness, drive more traffic to our blogs, make more sales, catapult our blogging careers and prosper!

10 STEPS TO BECOMING A WEALTHIER FREELANCE WRITER

Gone are the days when being a freelance writer meant that you were barely scraping by, trying to make ends meet, working at all odd hours of the night, having nightmares because you couldn't make enough to support yourself much less your family.

It was bad if you were a writer, not to mention if you were a *freelance* writer! That made it worse! But thanks to internet technology those days are long gone. Now, freelance writers can command very descent incomes. We can live comfortably, and we can even afford to take vacations! Very luxurious vacations too.

But for some freelance writers, there is still that doubt about whether one can actually become wealthy as a freelance writer. Well, I am here to tell you that your doubts are holding you back. Just do a survey and see how many freelance writers out there are making incomes that make many employed persons green-eyed with envy.

I want to talk about 10 things that freelance writers can do to become a wealthier freelance writer. Now wealth means many different things to many different people. In this case, when I say wealthy, I mean that your income is sufficient to cover all your expenses with money left to spare to enjoy the luxuries of life. I don't necessarily mean filthy, stinking, rolling in it. I just mean living comfortably enough to be able to help others out financially if necessary and to treat yourself every now and then.

So, here are the 10 things that you can do to change your financial circumstances as a freelance writer.

1. **Get Organized** – This single factor can help you to increase your income as a freelance writer many times over. As a freelance writer, your greatest resource is time. And those who use it wisely are the ones who usually become wealthy. Because as they say, time is money! Getting organized means that you should first of all establish a goal for yourself as a freelance writer. How much income do you desire to earn this year? Use that as your starting point to plan your monthly, weekly and daily activities. At the end of everyday, you should have accomplished a targeted set of objectives. Use time management tools and apps such as Pomodero, Evernote, Wunderlist etc to help you stay focused and organized. Remember that every minute wasted is money that you are throwing away!

2. **Respect the Writing Profession** – Are you one of those freelance writers who does it just because you have to? Or do you really and truly love to write? Whether you accept it or not, freelance writing is a very noble profession that deserves utmost respect. Don't treat the profession like it is something you would rather not do and expect it to make you wealthy! It's not going to happen. Only when you start respecting the profession, embracing it as a worthwhile and valuable undertaking, will you begin to realize the great earning potential of a career as a freelance writer. Begin to view yourself as a valuable person who has a great gift and talent that people are willing to pay top buck for.

3. **Review your rates** – If you charge minimum rates, you will never become a wealthy freelance writer. It's as simple as that. Set your

rates based on the value that you will be imparting to clients. One article that you write for a client can bring in hundreds or even thousands of dollars for that client. So don't underestimate the value of your work. Don't be afraid to ask for what you are worth. Ensure that your rates are not based on a poverty mentality. This brings me to the next point concerning attitude.

4. **Change Your Attitude** – According to famous author and motivational speaker, Randy Gage, 3 signs that you have a poverty mentality are a constant fixation on money, a resentment for rich and wealthy people and fear-based decision making. As a freelance writer who wants to become wealthy, a poverty mentality can hold you back and prevent you from realizing your full potential. Stop worrying about money so much and focus instead on improving the quality of your work on an ongoing basis. Focus on providing value to your clients on every single occasion. The money will follow.

5. **Become a Better Writer** – This means that you should be prepared to invest in yourself and in your career as a freelance writer. The best and most financially successful freelance writers are constantly learning new writing skills and improving their writing. There are several courses available both online and offline which are designed to make you a better writer. Avoid becoming complacent and refrain from thinking that you know it all. Because the truth is, you don't. Nobody knows it all. Udemy, for example, offers several affordable, online courses on writing. When you improve your writing, you have the right to demand higher rates and to be paid according to your level of expertise.

6. **Become Better at Marketing** – Marketing is an area that several freelance writers tend to ignore or to not do very well at. As a freelance writer, unless you have the resources necessary to pay someone to market on your behalf, you have to be prepared to market yourself and your writing. One of the best ways to market yourself as a freelance writer, is to start a blog and maintain it. It is really not as difficult as you may believe. But it does require time and commitment. In addition, you should establish an online presence in social media to raise awareness about your services. If no one knows that you are an excellent freelance writer, they will never hire you. Social media management tools such as Hootsuite and Buffer can help you effectively manage your social media marketing.

8. **Review Your Market** – As a freelance writer, it is important that you target your writing to the right audience. In order to do this however, you need to know your market and what their needs and desires are. Then you

should tailor your writing to match what is being demanded by people who need the services of a writer. The mistake that many freelance writers make is to just write without conducting any sort of research about the needs of the market first and then find that their messages fall on deaf ears. For example, there is always a need for copywriters and people are prepared to pay top dollar for top notch web content. The markets in which there is lots of demand, should be the markets that you focus on penetrating. There is no sense spending your time marketing creative writing services to a group of people who are not interested in creative writing. The key is to find the correct market and to market yourself where the demand is greatest.

9. **Offer Better Service Than Everybody Else** – I cannot emphasize enough, the importance of offering a top notch service to your customers. Because the fact is, that there is lots of competition out there in the world of freelance writing. You need to stand out if you hope to become a wealthy freelance writer. And it doesn't necessarily mean that you have to write better than the other person, it means that you have to offer more value to your customers. If you and your competitor both charge the same rate, your service should stand out based on the fact that you offer more for the same amount as your competitor. If, for example, you are offering copywriting services, you may want to offer something like a free consultation to add value to the deal. Be creative and you will find ways and means of standing out from the competition. Customer service is very important!

10. **If it Doesn't Work, Fix it!** – If you have been doing something and you find that it isn't working, don't be afraid to fix it. If you do what you did, you will get what you got! When I first began my freelance writing career, I was charging minimum fees and putting in maximum hours. As you probably imagine, I was stressed out and hardly earned anything to show for it. So I did some introspection and realized that if I wanted to earn more, I would have to charge more. If I wanted to work fewer hours and still make a great income, I would have to find a way to earn more on an hourly basis. So, I put every single one of the above 9 steps into place and today, I am a happy freelance writer. It's hard to match the feeling you get when you get a message that "your account has been loaded" and you don't have to run to withdraw the cash!

ESTABLISHING YOUR FREELANCE WRITING RATES

Your income as a freelancer hinges greatly on your freelance rates. As a new freelancer, it can sometimes be difficult to decide what rates to charge a client. This is one of the aspects of freelancing that requires some amount of thought and can be daunting if you have never had to set rates for your expertise before. As a freelancer you offer services that clients need and that they should be willing to pay for. The problem is that there are some clients who believe that because you are a freelancer that you should give away your services for free. Well, excuuuuse me, you are a freelancer but your services are definitely NOT for free! But how exactly do you decide what rates to charge a client? Many freelancers struggle with this decision; not wanting to charge to much in fear that they will lose the sale or on the other hand, not wanting to charge too little so that they end up working virtually for free. This chapter will help you to establish a freelance rate that is comfortable for you and that will allow you to earn a decent living as a freelancer. If you have ever wanted to know how to set your freelance rates without giving away your services for free, then go ahead and read the entire article now or bookmark it so that you can read it more thoroughly later on. Before we go any further, just know that whatever services you have to offer as a freelancer, that your services are valuable and that you are worth just as much or even more than a salaried employee would be worth. Don't think for a minute that because you are a freelancer that your services are somehow less than the services of an employee who is dedicated to a single employer. Once you establish that in your mind then you are ready to establish your freelance rates. Bear in mind that freelance rates are dependent on several factors including:

6. Industry
7. Location
8. Level of freelance experience

9. Level of industry experience
10. Qualifications
11. Market conditions

Start with the End in Mind

When establishing your freelance rates, you should start with the end in mind. Decide how much you would like to earn on an annual basis. The amount should be sufficient for you to cover all your personal and business expenses and enough profit that will allow you to live the lifestyle that you want including having a considerable amount of savings. This is essentially establishing a freelance budget.

Bear in mind all the expenses that you would need to cover for your freelance business including income taxes, utilities, supplies, travelling costs, marketing expenses etc. It may be useful to start by first coming up with the "take home" salary that you would want. This is the amount that you would consider to be your personal salary and it should be able to cover your personal expenses (groceries, childcare costs, etc) and leave enough for savings. After you have established that figure, you should then add on another amount that will adequately cover all business-related expenses including income taxes for the year. The total would be the annual income that you desire to make.

Decide how many hours you plan on working each day and how many days of the week you will be working. If for example, you plan to work 6 hours per day, 5 days per week , that would total 30 hours per week or 120 hours per month. For 12 months that would be a total of 1,440 hours (12 months x 120 hours) per annum. Let's say you determined that you want your total annual salary to be $80,000.00, your hourly rate would be found by dividing that $80,000 by 1,440 hours to total approximately $56 per hour.

After you have come up with your ideal freelance rate, you then need to do some research to adjust your rates to take other factors into account. When you have looked at the different factors and how they affect your freelance rates, you should be prepared to make adjustments as necessary

.Industry Freelance Rates

As a freelancer, your rates should be set based on the industry or industries that you serve. Typically, each industry pays differently based on the services required. For example, if you are a freelance writer serving the health industry, your rates would be different from a freelancer who is serving the technology or the financial industry. Similarly, a freelancer who offers creative services such as website design services or logo design services may need to incorporate material costs into their freelance rates. So, when deciding upon a freelance rate, you should research to find out what the going rate is for services in that particular industry.

My advice would be to avoid looking only at freelance rates in the freelance market but to make your search broader to include industry rates on a whole. The reason for this is that you want to get an idea of what salaried workers are being paid to fulfill the same services that you would fulfill for your client. Looking at freelance rates within the freelance market alone is certain to yield rates that are at the lower end of any pay or salary scale. If you offer valuable services, then you want to price your services accordingly and not based solely on what other freelancers are charging.

Just like a typical job search, you would need to have an idea of what the going market rate is. If you are just getting into freelancing then you need to find out the going rates for corresponding entry level positions within the industry. A simple google search is likely to return some valuable information. Avoid using the word "freelance" when you conduct your search so that the results include broad industry information. Also, speaking with other more experienced freelancers will give you valuable insight into the going rates.

So let's say that you are a freelance writer serving the retail clothing fashion industry in the United States. Your Google search may involve typing the keywords "fashion copywriter salary" into Google search. The results that are returned would be broad and would include salaries for different states in the US or salaries in other locations based on your Google search settings. You should research all the salaries for the locations that you intend to target. Take note of the level of experience and the level of expertise that is required for the position. Most listings would return an annualized salary or a salary based on hourly rates. Expect the salaries to vary by location. If you are not serving the US market then your search would be similar but you should include the geographic location that you are targeting as a part of the search. This would give you a good idea of what employers are paying for these services. Take careful note of the mean or the median salary. This figure will form the base of your freelance rate. Look at the salaries over a range of different organizations to get a solid idea of what the market standards are in that particular industry.

How Location Affects Freelance Rates

Your location as a freelancer as well as the location of your client should play a part in how you establish your freelance rates. As explained previously, different locations pay differently. For example, positions in New York generally pay higher than positions in other states. Similarly, if you land a job with a client outside of the United States, the rates of pay may vary tremendously. This is based on the general economy of the location and the value that is placed on that particular service at that specific location. You should try to get a general idea of the level of pay in the locations to which you would like to offer your services.

On the other hand, you shouldn't let your own location negatively affect your freelance rates. Just because you may live in a location where salaries are low in general, does not mean that you should set low freelance rates for yourself if you offer a valuable, in demand service. Do not allow your freelance rates to be limited by where you originate from especially if you offer your services online. Clients sometimes seek out freelancers from certain locations because they view it as a way of getting cheap labor. But the clients are not so much to blame for this. It is the freelancers who tend to set their freelance rates so low in general, that the location takes on the reputation of being a cheap labor market.

Avoid being put in a box and set your rates based on the value of the services that you offer. If other freelancers with similar qualifications and experience from other locations are landing higher rates of compensation, there is no reason why you shouldn't be able to attract similar rates. So while you should be cognizant of the fact that freelance rates differ based on location, don't allow that to be a limiting factor. This is especially true if the location where you offer your services generally pay higher rates to freelancers. For example, if your client is from the United States and you are based in India, don't be tempted to settle for low rates just because pay tends to be on the low end in India when compared to the US. If the client values the services that you offer, they should be prepared to compensate you just as well as they would compensate an equally qualified and equally experienced freelancer from their native country.

The Effect of Experience and Qualifications on Freelance Rates

The more experienced and the more qualifications you have as a freelancer, the higher you should set your rates. Also, the amount of experience you have prior to becoming a freelancer, should be taken into consideration. This means that each year that you operate as a freelancer, you should review your freelancer rates to account for the fact that you have added another 12 months of experience to your work history. What this should mean is that you should be now better qualified and better equipped to help your clients having learned new skills and acquired new knowledge during the preceding year. Therefore, you should be more valuable and your rates should reflect this increase in value. Any freelance rate increase that you give yourself should at least account for inflation and a further percentage depending on how much new knowledge and new skills you may have acquired during the year. So if the inflation rate is 6% and you gained new certification throughout the year, you may consider increasing your rates by about 12% to account for these factors.

On the other hand, if you are new to freelancing, you should consider starting at lower freelance rates until you have built up a reputation as a valuable freelancer. This doesn't mean that you should under-price your services, but be prepared to accept lower rates to get your feet in the door. Then slowly build from there based on how well your customers rate your services and on how in demand your services are.

Market Conditions and their effects on Freelance Rates

It goes without saying that any freelance rates that you set should be done taking market and economic conditions into consideration. If the demand for your particular type of services is high, this is an opportunity to increase your rates. On the other hand, if the demand is low, you should consider adjusting your freelance rates accordingly to help to boost sales. Look at what is happening in the economy in general also. A sluggish economy means that your services may be less in demand and that potential clients may be less able to afford your services. Be flexible to avoid losing business.

At the end of the day establishing your freelance rates requires lots of thought and research and should be revised on a regular basis.

HOW TO TURN $5 INTO A FORTUNE ON FIVERR

If you are an online freelancer, you've probably heard about Fiverr. It's that online freelancer platform that allows freelancers to offer their services to prospective buyers for as low as $5 per gig (job). I know that there are great misconceptions out there about Fiverr as an online freelancer platform. But don't be fooled by the seeming lack of earning potential of the platform because of the $5 gigs. In my opinion Fiverr is, hands down, the best online freelancer platform available. I'll explain why I say this in a moment. First, I want to just dispel the notion that an online freelancer who does business on Fiverr is poorly paid and scraping for pennies. Don't believe that for another second. Don't judge the platform if you've never offered your services there before. Some Fiverr sellers have quit their corporate jobs and are making full-time incomes with Fiverr. Not to mention sellers such as Chris Hardy who bought a house from his Fiverr revenues. Any online freelancer can turn $5 into a fortune on Fiverr. First let's discuss why I believe Fiverr is a great choice for any online freelancer

Fiverr is a Great Choice for any Online Freelancer

Let me first point out that I have an active seller account on Fiverr and I also buy services there are well. Here are the reasons why I think the platform is an excellent choice for business if you are an online freelancer:

- **The opportunity to package services to maximize income –** This feature is what makes the Fiverr platform unique and lucrative. If an online freelancer knows how to package his or her services right, they have the opportunity to earn much more than $5 from any single gig. After making your first 10 sales and getting good reviews, every freelancer has the opportunity to offer 'gig extras' which are additional services to complement the basic gig service. A gig extra can be something as simple as offering to do an express order at an additional charge. If online freelancers can think of all the different things they can offer with a single service to make their service unique and attractive, they have found a way to maximize their income. The key is to offer just the basic service for the $5 gig and to offer added value with gig extras. By so doing, an online freelancer on Fiverr can earn hundreds of dollars from a single order. Let's look at an example from the viewpoint of a freelance writer that offers article writing for a basic gig. Gig extras for this service can be such things as express service, SEO optimization of all articles, additional words, submission to article directories, sourcing of royalty-free images etc. You just have to get creative and break down whatever service you offer into bite size pieces that add extra value to the basic service. If this is done well, you can increase the average sale up from $5. In addition to ordering the basic gig, buyers have the opportunity to purchase whichever gig extra they need. Another plus is that it is possible for buyers to order multiple gigs per order. This makes the earning potential even greater for online freelancers.

- **No Bidding Required** – This is my second favorite feature of the platform. You do not have to bid on jobs in order to obtain work. Bidding for jobs is time-consuming and in my opinion is not fun. To spend my time submitting bids for jobs is something that I would rather not have to do as an online freelancer. I would rather spend that time completing jobs and earning money. While other platforms such as Elance and Odesk require that you submit bids for each and every job of interest, Fiverr has no such requirement. You simply create a winning profile, optimize it for the Fiverr's search engines and wait for the queries or the orders to come in. Now, don't get me wrong. It sounds simplistic but it isn't easy to stand out among the thousands of other sellers who are offering similar services as you are. And it does take some effort and skill to be able to attract queries and job orders. But once you get it right, you will have an inbox full of queries and/or orders each morning. What I like about this is that Fiverr gives the online freelancer the upper hand. After all, it is the buyers who are seeking the services of the professionals on Fiverr and they have the opportunity to submit queries to as many freelancers as they see fit. The online freelancer then has the option of accepting or rejecting a job query or job order or submitting a custom quotation in response to a job query. If the freelancer finds that he doesn't have any job orders or job queries, he/she has the option of submitting 'bids' in response to buyer requests posted on the platform. However, it is not mandatory for the freelancer to take part in this process. It is a choice that the freelancer is free to make.

- **The ability for a single freelancer to offer several different gigs** – Again, this is a feature that I love about the Fiverr platform. Whereas other online freelancer platforms may limit you to a single category, Fiverr places no such limitations on freelancers. If you are skilled at graphic design and you are also an excellent writer, there is ample opportunity for you to offer both services on Fiverr under the same username. I remember trying to offer more than one type of service on another online platform, and I was restricted to offering my services in a single category only. Not cool.

- **The ability to pause your gig and take a vacation** – Everybody gets tired and needs a vacation at some point in time. Fiverr allows online freelancers the freedom to take vacations as they see fit and necessary. During this time, their gig is still active within the offer stream but buyers will receive a notice that the freelancer is on vacation if they try to place an order or make a query. The notice will also inform the buyer of when the freelancer will resume working and the option to be notified as soon as the freelancer is back on the job. Fiverr still allows the freelancer to receive messages during this time so that they are kept in the loop about any activity taking place on their account while on vacation.

- **Benefit from the traffic already generated on the Fiverr platform** – While as a freelancer you may have your own blog from which you offer your services, having an account on Fiverr allows you to benefit from the traffic that the site already generates. It can take individual bloggers some time to generate enough traffic to their blog or website to garner sufficient orders. By having a presence on the Fiverr platform, freelancers can get added exposure to qualified leads and prospects who are ready to buy.

A Few tips for the online freelancer

Here are a few tips for you as an online freelancer on Fiverr.

- Make your service into a product. For example, if you offer the writing of press releases as your basic gig, you can create a PDF list of 100 free and 100 paid press release sites and offer that as a gig extra. Any service can be made into a product with a little creativity.

- Automate the completion of the gig service where possible. Although you should offer customized jobs to buyers, it is possible to come up with a standard 'template' upon which custom features may be easily added. This makes it possible to cut down on both the time and effort required to offer customized services.

- Spend time to create a great profile which should include live portfolio samples

- Offer excellent service at all times and you should receive great reviews

- Offer free order revisions – you owe it to the customer to get their order done right. That's what they are paying you for.

- Browse the forums now and then to see what is happening with other sellers

With a little effort and commitment, any online freelancer can turn $5 into a fortune on Fiverr. Go for it!

HOW TO ESTABLISH A FREELANCE BUDGET

Don't let the fact that you earn an unstable income keep you from establishing a freelance budget. If you are a freelancer, are self-employed or earn on a commission basis, your income is very likely to fluctuate to some extent. As someone who has an unstable income, I have found that it is not always easy to establish a freelance budget, much less follow one. While it can be very difficult to budget in such a situation, with some discipline and a determination to succeed, it is possible to establish and follow a freelance budget that will bring some order to your financial situation.

Earning on a commission basis or being self-employed has its perks. For one, you have the potential to earn as much or as little as your performance dictates. You are not restricted by a set pay check and your ability to exceed established goals and targets means that you can usually earn more than the regular salaried employee. Any salesperson or freelancer who has made huge bonuses for making those extra sales, knows how great it feels to be in charge of their own financial destiny. However, if you are such a salesperson or freelancer, you also know that when sales aren't happening as you'd like them to, you can begin to worry about how to make ends meet when your income falls short and threatens to blow your freelance budget.

Self-employed individuals and freelancers need to appreciate the fact that with performance based compensation comes the need for added financial discipline. Money management now takes on increased significance since your financial destiny is largely in your own hands and a freelance budget becomes a must. Managing a freelance budget while you have an unstable income therefore requires strict discipline and organization. Here are the main things you need to consider when budgeting on an unstable freelance income:

- **Pay attention to your Freelance Income** – Unlike regular employees who have an established salary and therefore need to pay less attention to income, you need to pay greater attention to your income. If you earn mainly based on your results rather than on your effort, it is important that you establish income goals for yourself. Studies have shown that goal setting involving the establishing of specific and challenging goals, results in better earning performance. Goal setting is a way of keeping yourself focused and motivated to achieve. Just like employed persons, you have regular expenses that you need to cover and you also have other financial goals that you would like to accomplish. Use this information as a guide in establishing an income estimate. I have heard many freelancers say that they don't set income goals because they have no control over how much they earn. This is far from the truth since you are the one who determines things such as your rates, your fees, your hours, who your clients are etc. These things should be taken into account when you establish your freelance budget.

- **Determine Your Average Freelance Income** – If you have been earning on a performance basis for 12 months or more, you can use this information to calculate your average monthly income. Add 15% to 20% to this figure to account for savings and unforeseen expenses and use the result as your minimum freelance budget income figure. If you have less than 12 months of past income information, you would need to estimate a figure that will allow you to cover all your expenses plus an additional 15% to 20% to cover miscellaneous expenses that you are not able to reasonably foresee. For example, if your regular monthly expenses amount to $2,000, you could add 20% to that figure to account for miscellaneous expenses and savings to arrive at a monthly estimate of $2,400. This income figure should be your goal on a monthly basis. In a circumstance where you don't have 12 months of income information, it is better to revise your income projections on a more regular basis based on the past month's results and your forecasts of the upcoming month. Do not be tempted to overestimate your income. It is better if you underestimate your income and overestimate your expenses.

- **Consider Seasonality** – In a situation where you have 12 months or more of income information on which to base your projections, you would have already taken seasonality into account when determining your average income. In the case where you don't have that information however, you need to account for seasonality based on your particular industry and the type of product or service that you offer. For example, if you are a freelance writer specializing in the event planning or wedding planning niche, you can reasonably expect that you will get more orders and therefore earn more during the months of June and December. Bear these things in mind when creating your freelance budget and plan accordingly especially if you have very little historical earnings information that you can use as a reasonable monthly income estimate.

- **Plan to save at least 10% of your freelance income** – When you are a freelancer or paid on a commission basis, it is easy to allow savings to take a back seat. On the contrary, saving become even more important for those persons who have an unstable income. Just like employed persons, you need to set aside at least 10% of your gross earnings as savings. While this may take a little added effort on your part, it is achievable. One way of doing this is by putting away 10% of every payment that you receive the moment that you receive it. So if you get a check for $500, you need to take out $50 and deposit that to a separate savings account. You can make this automatic by asking your bank to transfer 10% of all your deposits to a dedicated savings account. When you earn from an employer, you can regularly transfer 10% to a separate savings account. I wish Paypal offered such a service to make it easier on freelancers. Whatever you need to do to ensure that you are saving, do it. It will be well worth it in the long run. If you perform exceptionally well with your freelance budget and your income surpasses your budgeted amount, be certain to save the additional amount and not be tempted to spend it. This amount can come in handy during periods of low earnings when you may need to make up your income. Since you have no way of determining *exactly* how much you will earn on a monthly basis, it is important that you establish a savings cushion.

- **Account for both recurring and non-recurring expenses in your freelance budget** – When you have expenses that recur on a regular basis, it is easy to remember to include them in your monthly budget. On the other hand, when you have quarterly or bi-annual or annual expenses, it is just as easy to forget to include them in your budget. Non-recurring expenses such as school fees, motor vehicle parts, annual subscriptions and such the like should be accounted for in your regular budget so that these expenses don't catch you unprepared when it's time to make your payment. Determine how much you would need to set aside on a monthly basis in order to be able to make payments at the required times. For example, if your annual membership subscriptions total $1,200, you would need to include $100 ($1,200 divided by 12 months) in your monthly budget so that you would have set aside enough over the 12 month period.

- **Revise your freelance budget regularly** – For persons who have an unstable income, it is necessary to revise your freelance budget more regularly than someone who makes the same amount on a regular basis. It is important that at the end of every budget period that you compare your actual income and expenses with your budgeted income and expenses. If your budgeting was done well, your actual figures should closely resemble your budgeted figures. If not, you may find that your freelance budget was way off. Use the end of the period to make the necessary adjustments. Determine where your forecasts were off and do your own analysis of the possible reasons for any significant differences. Remember to take into account things that will affect your upcoming projected income such as expected economic changes, industry changes, regulatory changes, changes in the spending power of you target market and so on. By reviewing and revising your freelance budget on a monthly basis, you are able to make better financial decisions.

Time to Establish a Freelance Budget

Having an unstable income should not be an excuse for not budgeting. On the contrary, since both your income and your expenses are subject to fluctuation, it is important that you budget to bring some kind of order to your financial situation. As a freelancer, it is mandatory that you establish a freelance budget if your finances are to be kept in order. Otherwise, you will find it extremely difficult to achieve your financial goals and you will find that you don't have a firm grip on your finances. If you are like me, and you like to be in control of your financial situation, establishing and sticking to a freelance budget will allow you to exercise some amount of financial control. While you cannot determine which way the economy will go, you can determine beforehand how much you need to earn to cover your needs and how much you should be spending in order to end each month in the black. Having an income that fluctuates doesn't mean that your finances should be in disarray. With discipline, determination, consistency and organization, you can budget and reach your financial goals as a freelancer. At the end of the day remember that a budget is only useful if executed.

BONUS RESOURCE: 100 WEBSITES THAT PAY WRITERS

There are several webmasters and website owners who neither have the time nor the expertise to write web content that is effective. I have put together a list of 100 websites that will actually pay you to write content on their behalf. I have been deliberate in only including those sites that compensate freelance writers well for their efforts. There are websites on the list that pay up to $5,000 per piece so this is some valuable real estate I am sharing with you. Without further ado, here is the list.

Websites that Pay for Written Content

1. Back to College - $55 up per article

   Offers Tips for adults going to college.

2. E-Commerce Insiders - $75 up per article

   Focuses on Retail e-commerce industry news & issues

3. The Introspectionist - $25 up per piece

   Women and feminine issues

4. Scary Mommy - $100 per article. Offers advice for Moms and funny parenting stories

5. iPhone Life Magazine $50 - $100/article. Accepts articles on iOS and iPhone issues

6. Salon - $100 up. Accepts articles on politics, social commentary, culture, lifestyle

7. Cosmopolitan - $100 per article. Accepts hilarious or interesting college experiences

8. Babble - $150 up/article. Accepts articles on parenting, home, relationships, work and travel

9. Polygon - $125 for 500 words. Accepts articles on the business of video games

10 The Christian Science Monitor - $200 - $225 per piece. Journalist news stories

11 iWorkWell $200 per article or more. Focuses on Human Resource issues

12 HowlRound $50 up per piece. Theatre and performance

13 Listverse $100 per article. Interesting, unusual things

14 A List Apart $200 per article. Web design

15 Photoshop Tutorials $50 - $200 per article. Photoshop

16 Digital Ocean - up to $200 per article. Tutorials about Linux and FreeBSD cloud hosting

17 A Fine Parent - $100 up per article. Parenting and child rearing

18 Great Escape Publishing $50 - $200 per article. The art of getting paid to travel

19 WOW Women on Writing $50 - $150 per piece. Women and writing

20 Work Online Blog $50 per article. Working online

21 College Humor $25 - $50 per article. Humorous college experiences

22 Cracked $100 - $200 per article. List style humorous articles

23 What Culture $25 - $500 per article. A wide range of subjects

24 Developer Tutorials $30 - $50 per article. Programming and design guides

25 Ceramics $25 - $950 per article. Articles about ceramics

26 Sitepoint – compensation not published. Articles on web development

27 InstantShift   Compensation based on quality and volume. Articles on   Design and development

28 The Dollar Stretcher   - $50 per 500 words. Articles on living better for less

29 Writers Weekly $40 - $60 per article. Success stories about freelance writing

30 Change Agent - $50 per article.   Written by adult students about a range of topics

31 Chicken Soup for the Soul $100 - $200 per story. True stories that inspire

32 Power for Living $125 - $375 per story. Stories that show the power of Christ at work

33 The Upper Room $25 per 250 words. Accepts Christian meditations

34 The Sun Magazine $100 - $2000 per piece. Accepts essays, interviews, fiction and poetry

35 AARP Magazine   Up to $1 per word. Issues that affect persons over 50 years old

36 Transitions Abroad $50 - $150 per article. Travelling, studying, living, working abroad

37 Boulevard $25 - $300 per piece. Poetry, fiction and non-fiction pieces

38 Carve Magazine $100 per piece. Accepts short stories and poetry

39 Money Crashers   Compensation not published. Accepts articles on personal finance

40 Wise Bread   Compensation not published. Accepts articles on personal finance

41 Make A Living Writing - $75 per blog post. Success stories on earning money through writing

42 Freelance Writing $25 per blog post   The craft of writing fiction, non-fiction and poetry

43 The Penny Hoarder $100 - $500 based on page views. Creative ways to earn, save and grow money

44 Doctor of Credit $50 per blog post. Accepts articles on credit issues

45   Dorkly $35 - $75 per article. Animes, drawings etc.

46   App Storm $60 per article. Popular apps

47   The Layout $50 - $150 per article. WordPress CMS

48   VPS Web Hosting $50 - $150 per article. VPS Web hosting

49   Viator Travel Blog $100 - $150 per article. Insider's view of travel

50   Boots N All $50 per article. Independent travel

51   Take Lessons - $50 per article. How to guides from teachers on music etc

52   Author Magazine $50 per article. Accepts articles on how to write

53   Write Naked $50 per article. Interviews, Publishing trends etc

54   Lawyerist $100 per article. An online magazine about law practice

55   Conspiracy Club $50 per article. The topic of conspiracy

56   Cash Money Life   Compensation not published. Personal Finance

57   The Establishment $125 - $500 per article. Marginalized individuals who succeed

58   Everyday Feminism $75 per blog post. Acceptance of fatness

59   Guide Posts   Compensation not published. Overcoming obstacles through faith

60   Lighthouse $100 per post. Submissions from blind writers on a variety of topics

61   xoJane   Compensation not published. Personal stories from a raw, honest perspective

62   The Atlantic   Compensation not published. Accepts non-fiction, fiction and poetry

63   Blog Her $50 per syndicated or assigned post. Social media, blogging, etc.

64   Cultures and Cuisines $200 per article. Food and culture

65   Dame Magazine   Compensation not published. Essays, op-eds & humorous pieces about women

66   Fund Your Life Overseas $75 per post. Personal experience on how expats survive abroad

67   IWA Wine Blog $50 per post. Wine

68   The Kernel   Compensation not published. The internet, technology, and life

69   Knitty $120 - $200 per post. Articles and tutorials about knitting

70   The Mix   Compensation not published. Choose from on a variety of interesting topics

71   OZY   Compensation not published. People, places, trends etc that are ahead of their time

72   Paste Magazine   Compensation not published. Movies, TV, videogames, comedy, books etc

73   Pretty Designs Compensation negotiable.   Hair, fashion, nails, food

74   Refinery29   Compensation not published. South Korean beauty, extreme bargain shopping etc

75   Saveur   Compensation not published. Food and travel

76   Upworthy   Compensation not published. Original stories that are unusual

77   Compose $200 per article   Accepts articles about databases

78   The Graphic Design School $100 - $200 per article   Photoshop, Illustrator and InDesign

79   Linode $250 per article   Tutorials and trending news about Linux

80   SlickWP $100 per article   Tutorials on Wordpress & Genesis Themes

81   Tuts Plus Compensation not published Tutorials   on   code,   web design, etc.

82   Word Candy $0.06 per wordWordPress CMS

83   WP Hub $100 - $200 per article   Reviews on WordPress themes, plugins

84   Audio Tuts Plus $50 per tutorial or tip   Mini-tutorials on web design, coding etc

85   American College of Health Care Sciences $50 per article. Wholistic health and wellness

86   WorldStart $15 - $35 per article. Computer tips

87   Techlabs $50 - $75 per tutorial   Tutorials on Adobe

88   Reverb Press   Compensation not published. News-based articles on politics, fashion etc

89   Smashing Magazine Compensation depends on length and quality. Web development and design

90   Matador $40 up per article. Cultures, and adventures around the world

91   Glo Holiday $30 per article Accepts article about travelling

92   The Expeditioner $30 per article Accepts article about travelling

93   Working Mother   Compensation not published Accepting   articles related to working moms

94   Vela Magazine Compensation not published Accepts   non-fiction written by women

95   RankPay $100 per article   SEO, social   media   and   content marketing

96   Scripted   Compensation not published Accepts specialist articles

97   Web Loggerz   Compensation is negotiable Technical   aspects   of WordPress

98   Edu Writers $7 - $15 per page   Academic   pieces   on   business, agriculture, etc.

99   Writer Access Up to $2 per word Based on your particular area of expertise

100 The Content Authority   Depends on length and quality   Wide range of topics decided on by clients.

Thanks so much for purchasing my book. I hope you received value and I take this opportunity to wish you all the best in your freelance writing career. Please leave me a review if you found this content valuable. Thanks!

Check out my other book: **WordPress for Beginners: Simple Guide to Blogging for Profit** Also visit me online at my blog at Wealth Create Online

ABOUT THE AUTHOR

Keesha Metcalfe is a full time Freelance Writer and Blogger with a background in Finance. She is passionate about helping others to make money using their writing talents. When she isn't writing, she enjoys travelling and spending time outdoors with family and friends. She is married and is mother to 3 adorable boys.

www.ingramcontent.com/pod-product-compliance
Lightning Source LLC
Chambersburg PA
CBHW070330190526
45169CB00005B/1829